THE LITTLE BOOK OF
CHELSEA

Independent and Unofficial

FIFTH EDITION

EDITED BY
CLIVE BATTY

First published by Carlton Books in 2003
Updated editions 2010, 2014, 2017

This edition published in 2021 by OH!
part of Welbeck Publishing Group
20 Mortimer Street, London, W1T 3JW

A CIP catalogue record of this book is available from the British Library.

ISBN 978 1 91161 034 2

Printed in Dubai

10 9 8 7 6 5 4 3 2 1

CONTENTS

INTRODUCTION

Forget *The Mousetrap*, the longest-running, most dramatic show in London is staged at Stamford Bridge. Reviews have been mixed over the years, but for jaw-dropping plot twists the multi-billion-pound production that is 'The Blues' simply can't be topped. Ecstatic highs, depth-plumbing lows, silverware and scandal, with an all-star cast drawn from the four corners of the globe, this show has the lot.

In this great collection of quotes, players, fans and managers reveal why, for them, Blue really is the colour. From the glory of the 1955 title and the glamour days of the 1970s, to the 18 major trophies the Blues have won in the Roman Abramovich era, there are soundbites to satisfy every Chelsea fan. Peter Osgood, Terry Venables, Dennis Wise, Ken Bates, John Terry, Didier Drogba, Diego Costa and Eden Hazard are all featured along with a host of great managers, from Gianluca Vialli and Carlo Ancelotti to Felipe Scolari, the incomparable Jose Mourinho, Antonio Conte and Frank Lampard.

Chelsea is London's undisputed glamour club – no wonder then that so many people have so much to say about it.

CHAPTER 1

WE LOVE CHELSEA

❝Life is never dull at Stamford Bridge.**❞**

KEN BATES

"Becoming a Chelsea director was one of the most marvellous things that has happened in my life."

LORD ATTENBOROUGH

" Of all the roles Chelsea are expected to fulfil – highest ticket prices in the league, snazziest restaurant, chairman with the most voluminous beard – winning the title is not one of them. **"**

JIM WHITE

journalist and Manchester United fan writing in October 1998
and no doubt still eating his words

❝I had one agent phoning up saying, 'I have the honour of representing one of the world's greatest players, he needs no introduction.' I said, 'You're right, I don't want to meet him.'**❞**

KEN BATES
keeps his chequebook shut, summer 2002

" Modern-day newspapers would have had a field day just following Chelsea around. We wouldn't have been off the front or back pages. **"**

DAVID WEBB

on the 70s side, November 2000

❝ Chelsea FC will never lose its identity. Chelsea will be Chelsea for always – and at Stamford Bridge. **❞**

BRIAN MEARS

Chelsea chairman at a time of financial crisis, April 1977

WE LOVE CHELSEA

Last Thursday we received a letter, dated next Monday, complaining about appalling language in the Shed at today's match against Everton. You have been warned!

KEN BATES

September 1991

❝Quite frankly there are some players here who are simply not good enough.**❞**

KEN BATES

May 1983

❝People still come up to me and say thanks for some fantastic memories. That really brings home that you've played a part in this club's great history. It really means something special.**❞**

KERRY DIXON

❝I've been coming to Chelsea for 55 years and it's one of the joys of my life. No matter what concerns I have about work or other matters, for that hour and a half watching out there, it's just magic. I absolutely love it.**❞**

LORD ATTENBOROUGH

" The day I walked through the door I just thought what a magnificent ground, magnificent stadium, fantastic name, and a tremendous location. Why isn't this club bigger than Arsenal and Spurs? **"**

KEN BATES

July 1977

❝I wanted to build an exciting new Chelsea, providing such entertainment that the players got a standing ovation from the fans even if they lost. **❞**

KEN BATES

outlines his football vision, May 1984

❝Matthew was always bubbly. He loved being amongst us. That's the way he'd want to be remembered, I reckon. A bubbly, nice, respected Chelsea supporter.**❞**

DENNIS WISE

pays tribute to Matthew Harding, October 1996

"When my team looked into clubs with the best possible fundamentals and prospects, Chelsea really did come first. The ground, the location, the Champions League qualification, the staff and players and fan support were, and remain, a wonderful foundation.**"**

ROMAN ABRAMOVICH

August 2003

" He might be a billionaire but he is already regarded as one of us – a Chelsea, or Chelski, Boy. **"**

KEN BATES

on Roman Abramovich, August 2003

❝I don't want to change what works. I just want to help take what we have at Stamford Bridge to the next level. And I want us all to work hard and have a lot of fun doing it.**❞**

ROMAN ABRAMOVICH

August 2003

"Without our fantastic supporters, there would not be a Chelsea Football Club and we will never forget that. In the future, we hope to bring you more joy than you have experienced in the last hundred years.**"**

ROMAN ABRAMOVICH

2005

❝By 2014 we want to be internationally recognised as the No. 1 club. It's a very ballsy vision but one that has captured the interest of the owner.**❞**

PETER KENYON

reveals the extent of Chelsea's ambition, November 2006

CHAPTER 2

HEROES OF THE SHIRT

"I didn't get that worked-up in the dressing room. Instead, I used to read the programme to see who I had to kick that week. **"**

RON "CHOPPER" HARRIS

❝Tommy Docherty and Ron 'Chopper' Harris invented soccer violence. It's when they retired that it spread to the terraces. **❞**

PETER OSGOOD

“Peter Osgood has never been replaced since the day Chelsea sold him.**”**

ALAN HUDSON

January 2001

"I like to think that, apart from being a bit of a butcher, I've something else to offer.**"**

RON "CHOPPER" HARRIS

1979

❝I never got sent any knickers, but girls would write to ask where I hung out in my spare time and whether I was courting.**❞**

GARRY STANLEY

1970s heart-throb

❝I'm a goalkeeper, so I expected the outfield players to gang up on me at some point. **❞**

PETER BONETTI

after being voted off a "footballers' special" edition of
The Weakest Link

"Leading Chelsea back to the First Division is the biggest thrill of my life.**"**

RAY WILKINS

May 1977

❝The worst crowd trouble I saw was down at Millwall. In the warm-up, there were people coming out of the crowd with meat-hooks in their heads. I think that's the only time I've been frightened in a game. **❞**

IAN BRITTON

recalls a terrifying trip to The Den in 1976

"The best Italian this club has signed is the chef."

FRANK LEBOEUF

January 1999

" Keep shooting.
Never be afraid to miss. **"**

KERRY DIXON

outlines his goal-scoring philosophy, February 1985

“Wisey said I think too much. But I have to do all his thinking for him.**”**

GIANFRANCO ZOLA

May 2001

" They call me 'The Radio' because I talk. I love talking. I can't help it. It's a family problem. My wife speaks a lot. My father's always talking. Sometimes at home we need to do a time-out, like in basketball, to stop everybody from talking. **"**

GUS POYET

May 2000

"It was a gamble to come to England but I saw what Ole Gunnar Solskjaer achieved and I thought, 'I can do better than that.'"

TORE ANDRE FLO

September 1997

"When Vinnie Jones and Mick Harford were in the same side you'd have needed crash helmets to play against them, never mind shin-pads.**"**

TOMMY LANGLEY

June 2002

"Quite simply, the little man is a genius."

DENNIS WISE

on Gianfranco Zola

❝I used to share a room with Gianfranco Zola but I had to throw him out because he snored so much.**❞**

ROBERTO DI MATTEO

February 1999

Ed de Goey is the worst-dressed man I've ever seen. One pair of jeans, one pair of trainers, one shirt and one haircut.

JOHN TERRY

December 2002

❝If he's not the best striker in Europe, I don't know where there's a better one. His all-round game is fantastic. He's scoring spectacular goals. That's Didi and it's great to have a striker playing like that.**❞**

An excited **FRANK LAMPARD**
acknowledges Didier Drogba's scintillating form, October 2006

"If I was having a race with my mum and I was expected to beat her by 50 yards, I'd like to be beat her by 60 yards.
I love winning.**"**

FRANK SINCLAIR

December 1996

"People will always say the best player at Chelsea has been Gianfranco Zola but I would say Peter was the greatest. He was such a strong player, a big fellow who scored goals and scared defenders.**"**

RON "CHOPPER" HARRIS

pays tribute to the late Peter Osgood, March 2006

"Sometimes it is good to score after 43 seconds… and sometimes it is better to last a little longer.**"**

ROBERTO DI MATTEO

"I am sure John Terry has got a hell of a future. The only difference between him and me is that, when I tackled, they didn't get up.**"**

RON "CHOPPER" HARRIS

May 2001

❝I have been here since I was 14 and to be made captain of such a great team is a dream come true.❞

JOHN TERRY

September 2004

"I think he's a fantastic captain because he's Chelsea through and through. He plays like he's got feelings for the club. **"**

Former skipper **RON "CHOPPER" HARRIS**
on John Terry, October 2004

❝I know full well that I'm not a greedy person. I've not come here for money. I've come here because I want to win things and I have a good chance of winning things at Chelsea.**❞**

ASHLEY COLE

signs from Arsenal, September 2006

❝I know I am not risking my life by playing again, and that is the main thing. **❞**

Brave **PETR CECH** *returns to action in January 2007, three months after a horrific head injury at Reading.*

❝It's an incredible achievement and my loyalty to Chelsea has paid dividends. It is a great club and I am fortunate to be the captain of a very good team.**❞**

JOHN TERRY

after leading Chelsea to four FA Cup wins, May 2012

"He is my hero. No striker I have ever played with has scored so many important goals in finals.**"**

FRANK LAMPARD

praises Didier Drogba after the 2012 FA Cup win

❝I feel good at this club, and I still have a lot of things to do here... I am certain of what I have in mind, where I'm going. No-one will change my mind. The objective is to be the best with Chelsea.**❞**

EDEN HAZARD

committing his long-term future to Chelsea in 2014

❝After Messi and Ronaldo, [Eden] Hazard is my favourite player. I love watching him because he is a player who creates things and it is often spectacular to see him play.**❞**

ZINEDINE ZIDANE

2015

If you want to achieve something, you must have a goal in life. In my case, being a football player was a dream. My real obsession was to give my family a better life, no matter what.

DIEGO COSTA

2015

I would like to wish Claudio Ranieri and Leicester congratulations from me. I am delighted they have won the league and I am glad Tottenham haven't.

JOHN TERRY

2016

"I don't care what anybody says, I don't listen to anybody. The only people I have to prove myself to is the manager of the football club that I'm playing at and my team-mates that I'm playing with.**"**

GARY CAHILL

2016

"You have to fight for your dream, but you also have to feel fortunate for what you have. **"**

CESC FABREGAS

❝To come to a new club, he has stepped up again and been tremendous this season. He works hard and is a humble guy off the pitch and on it he is phenomenal.**❞**

GARY CAHILL

on N'Golo Kante, who joined Chelsea in 2016 and won the
Premier League title in 2017

❝ It's not the way I wanted to leave, ever. I have special affection for the people at Chelsea. I'm not a person who is going to smear the image. They know the person I am. **❞**

DIEGO COSTA

shows his love for the Blues ahead of leaving the club in January 2018

❝I was amazed by his speed of execution, he is the player I played against this year who impressed me the most. **❞**

KYLIAN MBAPPE

the French star says Eden Hazard was his best opponent in 2018

"Hazard is the most skilful player that's ever played for Chelsea, and that's saying something because look at the quality of players that they've had. He's astonishing.**"**

PAT NEVIN

the ex-Chelsea star praises Eden Hazard after the 2019 Europa League final

CHAPTER 3

GAFFER TALK

" The pressure for me is not important.
I was born with pressure. **"**

ANTONIO CONTE

2016

"Seeing this side develop has been like planting a seed and watching it grow like a flower.**"**

EDDIE McCREADIE

February 1977

"I was like Red Adair, saving the team from the drop. But I knew it would only be until the end of the season.**"**

DAVID WEBB

on his brief spell as Blues boss in 1993

❝It might be poor old Chelsea,
or dear old Chelsea, but that's better
than no Chelsea at all, isn't it?**❞**

Blues boss **DANNY BLANCHFLOWER**

February 1977

"In Italy I liked to say the manager is like a tailor. You have to best dress the team.**"**

ANTONIO CONTE

2016

❝I don't buy a player for his entertainment, because then you're going to work in a circus. **❞**

RUUD GULLIT

August 1997

ff We're slightly underrated maybe, and I
hope that there is a small flame flickering
that can grow into a blazing inferno. **JJ**

ANTONIO CONTE

2016

"All those bankers earning hundreds of thousands of pounds a year in the City would give it all up for 15 minutes playing for Chelsea.**"**

LAWRIE SANCHEZ

former Fulham boss

"I will say that after every game, the press ask me about the passion of Diego Costa, about his behaviour. Today I can say he had fantastic behaviour to control the situation, because he took a lot of kicks…I'm pleased because he showed me, he showed his teammates and he showed everyone that he had fantastic behaviour, and it wasn't easy.**"**

ANTONIO CONTE

2016

❝When Ruud made it clear that
he wanted a package that would cost
us £3.7m plus bonuses we knew it was
the end of the road. **❞**

KEN BATES

on the sacking of Ruud Gullit, February 1998

❝We had to make a change. There is no easy way to do it. Do you go for a shot in the head, or a death from a thousand cuts?**❞**

KEN BATES

on the sacking of Gianluca Vialli, September 2000

❝I can look back and say, 'I've lived,' and that's all down to this old funny game.**❞**

GIANLUCA VIALLI

February 2000

“ When I got sacked by Chelsea,
I didn't realise how much it would hurt. **”**

JOHN HOLLINS

November 1997, nine years after Ken Bates gave him his P45

"You may not have heard of me
before I came to you last month,
but I had heard of you.**"**

CLAUDIO RANIERI's

message to Chelsea fans, October 2000

"I feel very akin to the English warrior spirit – the spirit of fighting for every ball.**"**

CLAUDIO RANIERI

May 2001

"I consider defeat to be a state of virtual death.**"**

ANTONIO CONTE

"I would be disappointed if he was leaving. I have enjoyed his company in the times we meet after the game and things like that. He has a good personality and I enjoy the competition against him.**"**

SIR ALEX FERGUSON

shows Jose Mourinho all due respect

" Chelsea deserve all the plaudits they will get and, especially on their home form, they are worthy champions. **"**

SIR ALEX FERGUSON

concedes Chelsea are worthy winners of a second successive title, April 2006

❝I am not 'the Special One'.
I'm the normal one, but my wife
says I am special. **❞**

Mourinho's successor **AVRAM GRANT**
makes a low-key entrance, September 2007

❝He had my full support. I'm sure
two or three of the other players
would say the same. **❞**

JOHN TERRY

hints at divisions in the Blues' camp after Luiz Felipe Scolari's sacking,
February 2009

"Ballack, Cech and Drogba became my enemies. Somehow, they have a direct line to Abramovich.**"**

LUIZ FELIPE SCOLARI

blames three senior players for his demise, February 2009

" He was a nice guy, happy with everybody, but if you can't get the results it's difficult. **"**

MICHAEL BALLACK

damns Scolari with faint praise, March 2009

"I really envy Ruud because he was so cool and calm. The way I am doing this job is a little bit different. I can't get away from thinking about football 24 hours a day.**"**

GIANLUCA VIALLI

February 1998

❝Jose is the best in the business, there's no doubt about that, and I am sure he will be for the next 20 years. That's what we want at Chelsea, the best and only the best. **❞**

Skipper **JOHN TERRY**
wants Mourinho to stay at the Bridge

"If Mourinho is Jesus, then I am certainly not one of his apostles.**"**

New Chelsea boss **CARLO ANCELOTTI**
reveals he's not a fan of his most famous predecessor, October 2009

❝I don't know if Chelsea miss him, but we don't miss him. He did a lot of damage against us. ❞

Arsenal's **ARSENE WENGER**

is glad to see the back of Didier Drogba, September 2012

❝I don't ever remember a player playing against a side I have managed as well as he did – no matter what we did we couldn't cope with him… we tried everything but there was nothing we could do.**❞**

Sunderland boss **GUS POYET**
on Eden Hazard, 2013–14 season

"My football is both application and fun. And if you're having fun, it's less tiring. I've come to realize there's a child in every footballer; a child who is playing a game. That's where the fun part is. And when players are having fun, they're more productive. **"**

MAURIZIO SARRI'S

coaching philosophy when appointed Chelsea boss in 2018

" Frank Lampard was an extraordinary football player and he will be an extraordinary manager. **"**

PEP GUARDIOLA

" I am not naive. I understand fans want success. I don't see this as a risk. I am not fearful of the downsides. **"**

FRANK LAMPARD

on expectations after being appointed Chelsea manager in July 2019

" Tammy is a personality that's growing in our dressing room every day with his enthusiasm and his will to win. He is a striker that's near the top of the goalscoring charts in the league, he's showing his all-round game, stretches defences and he starts our press. **"**

FRANK LAMPARD

reflecting on Tammy Abraham's growing influence at Chelsea after coming back from injury in December 2019

" He is getting a more complete striker now and is learning a lot. He is a fantastic signing for Chelsea and he is only happy when he scores, so I hope he is unhappy after the game. **"**

Southampton boss **RALPH HASENHUTTL**
talks about Timo Werner ahead of a 2020 clash with the Blues

CHAPTER 4

THE SPECIAL ONE SPEAKS

"Please don't call me arrogant, but I'm a European champion and I think I'm a special one.**"**

JOSE MOURINHO

on his arrival at Chelsea, June 2004

❝I was not happy about these stories about me wanting an English passport and Sven's job. It was all ridiculous. **❞**

JOSE MOURINHO

rules himself out of contention to be the next England manager, October 2005

103

" All of my players were magnificent and deserved to win, no doubt. We now have the first title and almost for sure we will have the second one. And that will be the big one. **"**

JOSE MOURINHO

*looks forward to more success after Chelsea's
Carling Cup triumph, February 2005*

"I think he is one of those people who is a voyeur. He likes to watch other people. There are some guys who, when they are at home, have a big telescope to see what happens in other families. He speaks, speaks, speaks about Chelsea.**"**

JOSE MOURINHO

has a pop at Arsene Wenger, October 2005

❝I am manager today, I am the manager until the end of the season and I believe I will be the manager until the end of 2010. If I believe what I read in the press there are 11 candidates for my job but I don't get influenced by that.**❞**

JOSE MOURINHO

responds to questions about his future
at Stamford Bridge, January 2007

❝My bad qualities are that I don't care about my image and because of that I don't care about the consequences of what I say and the consequences of what I do.**❞**

JOSE MOURINHO

candid as ever, December 2006

"It was a beautiful and rich period of my career. I want to thank all Chelsea FC supporters for what I believe is a never-ending love story.**"**

JOSE MOURINHO

after he left Chelsea by "mutual consent" in September 2007

" When I look at that team only Ivanovic and Anelka are not players from my time. So it's a team without secrets for me. "

JOSE MOURINHO

claims Chelsea are still "his team" ahead of the Blues'
clash with Inter Milan, January 2010

"This time I will go back to a different dressing room, a different dugout but I know Mourinho is normally lucky at Stamford Bridge.**"**

JOSE MOURINHO

looks forward to his return to SW6
with Inter Milan, February 2010

❝ Chelsea have suffered in the last two years, and it's no coincidence that this decline happened after I left. **❞**

JOSE MOURINHO

as modest as ever, February 2010

❝If Roman Abramovich helped me out in training we would be bottom of the league and if I had to work in his world of big business, we would be bankrupt!**❞**

JOSE MOURINHO

during his first spell as manager

"I don't want to win the Europa League. It would be a big disappointment for me. I don't want my players to feel the Europa League is our competition.**"**

It's the Champions League or nothing for **JOSE MOURINHO**
July 2013

❝He is a specialist in failure… eight years without a piece of silverware, that's failure. If I did that in Chelsea I'd leave and not come back to London.**❞**

JOSE MOURINHO

blasts Arsene Wenger, February 2014

❝I am not the kind of guy that makes life easy for the great players. If they are great they have to give more than the others. If they are great they cannot be happy with a few good things they do. As a manager this is the last kind of player that I praise.**❞**

JOSE MOURINHO

2014

"Boring are a team who play at home and cannot score a goal.**"**

JOSE MOURINHO

December 2013

❝When you are the type of personality that puts pressure on yourself, I don't think you need to be worried about anything else.**❞**

JOSE MOURINHO
November 2013

" The world has plenty of special ones –
but I was the first. **"**

JOSE MOURINHO

November 2013

❝I feel like I had a hand in getting Jose Mourinho fired… I made a joke at the GQ awards in London where Mourinho was receiving some sort of special award... and I made a crack like, 'I love your style, seven men in the box, defensive soccer, keep it going.' And then next thing you know [he's fired], I'm so sorry.**❞**

WILL FERRELL

feeling guilty about his part in getting the special one sacked

CHAPTER 5

MAGIC CHELSEA

❝I was so happy to hear those Chelsea cheers. I could have wept. That wonderful crowd. They had been taking it on the chin for 50 years and always come up smiling. How well they deserved to have something to cheer about now.**❞**

Captain **ROY BENTLEY**

after Chelsea's first Championship win, April 1955

"I'd say the 1997 FA Cup Final
was the highlight of my Chelsea career,
just because it was such a long time since
we'd won a trophy and it meant that people
were talking about that team rather than
previous Chelsea teams.**"**

STEVE CLARKE

February 2002

" *Brutissimi!* Terrible! It was one of the worst games of my life! **"**

Manchester United goalkeeper **MASSIMO TAIBI**
recalls the Blues' 5–0 win in October 1999

"Q: What time is it?
A: Five past United! **"**

KEN BATES

cracks a joke after the same game

"I believe the last man to score five times in a Chelsea shirt was David Mellor.**"**

TONY BANKS MP

July 1997

"Yoghurts are down at Asda.**"**

GRAEME LE SAUX

when asked for his "Save of the Month", September 1998

"I think Luca dropped it, and then tried to blame it on me! I'm not quite sure who dropped it, actually. It wasn't me, honest!**"**

DENNIS WISE

explains a dent in the lid of the FA Cup, November 2000

❝The day at Bolton when we won the League will always be special, but to get my hands on the trophy at Charlton and lift it, it was the best thing in my life so far.**❞**

JOHN TERRY

reflects on Chelsea's Premier League title triumph, September 2005

❝The appointment of Jose Mourinho is all about building on the foundations which we have already established at Chelsea. His record of sustained success makes him perfect for what we want to achieve.**❞**

Chelsea chief executive **PETER KENYON**
June 2004

❝Stand up for the special one.**❞**

CHELSEA FANS

chant in appreciation of Jose Mourinho

"It's a massive achievement. United have dominated this league for a while, but now we're putting down our marker and proving that we're capable of doing that. **"**

JOE COLE

relishes Chelsea's second Premier League title, 2006

132

"He simply was the most successful Chelsea manager ever, and the best manager I have ever worked with.**"**

JOHN TERRY

pays tribute to Jose Mourinho, September 2007

133

"It was one of the biggest achievements of my career, winning in the Mecca of world football.**"**

GUUS HIDDINK

signs off his brief stint as Blues boss with victory in the FA Cup Final against Everton at Wembley, May 2009

❝It's an incredible achievement by this group of players. A lot of people had written us off but we showed again what kind of character these players have.**❞**

ROBERTO DI MATTEO

after beating Barcelona to reach the final of the
2012 UEFA Champions League

ff This is right up there, the way we've finished the season in such style. We deserved to come out on top. The first two titles we won relatively easily. They were very special because they were the first ones, but with the difficulties we've had this year, that was very, very special. **,,**

FRANK LAMPARD

on the 2009–10 Premier League title, May 2010

❝This feels magnificent. It's been three hard years seeing Manchester United lift it. We've got it back now and we need to do what United have done and maintain this success for a few years. **❞**

JOHN TERRY

after winning the 2009–10 Premier League title

"They're crying. It was Drogba, it was the angels, it was the heavens, it was the stars, it was the gods, it was everything for Chelsea. This is not anything to do with football. This is more than football, this is spirit. Never giving in, fighting to the end, that English spirit running right the way through this Champions League for Chelsea.**"**

GARY NEVILLE's

punditry after Chelsea won the
2012 UEFA Champions League Final

" It was written a long time ago that Chelsea were going to win. The cup is going back to Stamford Bridge and it is the best feeling ever. **"**

DIDIER DROGBA

after winning the 2012 UEFA Champions League

"For me to win in my first season in England, I am really proud of the achievement. My players showed me great professionalism, commitment, work-rate and will to try to win this league. **"**

ANTONIO CONTE

celebrates the Premier League title in May 2017

" We had some ups and downs but we have improved a lot and learned a lot this season. We finished well and won a trophy. It is my third title in Europe with Chelsea, they believe in my game. **"**

DAVID LUIZ

after the Blues beat Arsenal 4–1 in the Europa League final in May 2019

CHAPTER 6

IT'S GREAT TO BE A BLUE

"I've played for some big clubs
but Chelsea were the tops.
I loved the place, still do.**"**

MICKEY THOMAS

❝I would love to relive those days at Chelsea – they were wonderful times.**❞**

JIMMY GREAVES

"Chelsea has always been my first love. I'd have liked to have spent the whole of my career at Stamford Bridge, but it was not to be. I always have a special place in my football heart for Chelsea.**"**

TERRY VENABLES

January 1991

" The Chelsea goal-posts have become my friends, next to all the fellows who have been my team-mates over the years. **"**

PETER BONETTI
April 1976

❝I had other offers but Mourinho is Mourinho. You can't reject him.❞

NEMANJA MATIC

2014

"Somehow it's always a better feeling when you put one in at the Shed end – you get such a roar from those fans.**"**

CLIVE WALKER

October 1978

"I am growing in a team that plays beautiful football, something which is important in my eyes. It would be a privilege to finish my career at a club as big as Chelsea. **"**

WILLIAN

2016

❝Chelsea play in white socks.
I always win things in white socks.**❞**

RUUD GULLIT

July 1995

" My biggest regret is that I never won
anything at Stamford Bridge.
I loved the club and still do. **"**

CLIVE WALKER

December 1994

" We had a fantastic story during my first time at the club. I always had a wonderful relationship with the fans and I am looking forward to wearing the blue shirt at Stamford Bridge once again. **"**

DAVID LUIZ

2016

❝It was laughable, no? I mean, how can the captain of Chelsea, in the middle of the season, leave the club? To go to Manchester? I mean, it's not possible…**❞**

MARCEL DESAILLY

on a rumoured move to Manchester United, April 2002

154

"I played for Napoli and it was blue.
I play for Chelsea and it's blue. Italy is blue.
Blue belongs to me, my life.**"**

GIANFRANCO ZOLA

January 2002

"Everybody is talking about Chelsea. Real Madrid is no different to anyone. There's lots of interest. Everybody is talking about the ambition of the London club, Chelsea.**"**

CLAUDE MAKELELE

September 2003

" After eight years here this is my home and there is no other place I would rather play football. **"**

BRANISLAV IVANOVIC

2016

"On paper we've got the best squad around, best manager and we're hungrier than anyone else. Put those three together and you'll never be far off. **"**

DAMIEN DUFF

anticipates more success, September 2005

"We are like soldiers going out to perform our duty. It is a big battle ahead and we have to conquer the enemy to move forward and succeed.**"**

MICHAEL ESSIEN

declares war on title rivals Manchester United, December 2006

" The fans are awesome, every player wants to play in a place where he is fully accepted and I've that here at Chelsea. **"**

A contented **DIDIER DROGBA**
November 2006

❝I do not know if he is a referee or a thief. There are no words to describe the person who was on the pitch there.**❞**

JOSE BOSINGWA

is unimpressed by Norwegian ref Tom Henning Ovrebo's performance in the Chelsea–Barcelona Champions League semi-final, May 2009

"It's a load of crap and you can quote me on that. **"**

UEFA General Secretary **DAVID TAYLOR**
bluntly dismisses talk of an anti-Chelsea conspiracy after the
Blues' controversial defeat by Barcelona, May 2009

❝I love this club. Those last eight years have been the best in my career and in my entire life. ❞

DIDIER DROGBA

May 2012

ffYou talk about the Zolas and the best players to have played at the club, but for me he [Lampard] is the best. **JJ**

JOHN TERRY

praises Frank Lampard's 200-goal tally

" Farewell Didier Drogba. You have enthralled us, occasionally enraged us, but always entertained us. A striking superstar. **"**

GARY LINEKER
on Twitter, May 2012

" Chelsea is my life, as it it yours.
The best moments of my life have
been in this stadium. **"**

JOHN TERRY

2016

"It's my dream to win the Champions League and I'm sure I can, playing for Chelsea.**"**

FERNANDO TORRES

January 2011

" We have to start with an intention to win. If I sat here and didn't say that then I shouldn't be here. We want to play Champions League football year in and year out. **"**

FRANK LAMPARD

sets obvious targets as Chelsea manager in July 2019

"As a young kid, I've always believed
I will play for Chelsea. I always believe
that. I think I have the ability to.
I just have to, when I get the opportunity,
grab it with two hands.**"**

TAMMY ABRAHAM

looking forward to the start of the 2019–20 season

“In every big club, there's competition, and it always motivated me to fight for my spot. **”**

OLIVIER GIROUD

insists he's not threatened by Chelsea signing Timo Werner

❝Thiago's influence has been huge; even without the language his professionalism has been very clear, that rubs off on players, they respect him… Long may it continue not just for him but for the influence he has on the team. **❞**

FRANK LAMPARD

on Thiago Silva

CHAPTER 7

CELEBRITY VIEWS

❝Chelsea were the natural team for me to support. I would catch the 45 bus from Loughborough Junction to Battersea Bridge, and then walk across the bridge. I'd supported them earlier, but I actually started going in the year they won the Championship, 1954–55.**❞**

JOHN MAJOR
August 1990

❝I played against Ron Harris
and he frightened the life out of me.
Thankfully, he never whacked me,
and I appreciate that. **❞**

Former Tottenham winger **PETER TAYLOR**

❝Skilful as he was, Ossie could dish it out and I was no shrinking violet. We hated each other with venom. **❞**

FRANK McLINTOCK

captain of Arsenal's 1971 Double-winning team

" What they say about footballers being ignorant is rubbish. I spoke to a couple yesterday and they were quite intelligent. **"**

RAQUEL WELCH

after a visit to the Bridge in 1973

❝ Hoddle was one of my idols and it would have been brilliant to link up with the likes of Ruud Gullit, Dennis Wise and Mark Hughes. **❞**

IAN WRIGHT

on a never-to-happen move to West London

❝I had a lot of offers but Chelsea were the
only club I would have signed for. **❞**

GEORGE BEST

(sadly the Blues couldn't afford his wage demands)

ffDad supported Arsenal but I was a Chelsea fan. I'll never forget the first game I saw. It was Chelsea at home to West Ham, and I remember Clive Walker was in the side. He was a player who excited me, and I couldn't wait to go back. **JJ**

PAUL MERSON

1995

❝I was a Chelsea fanatic. When my turn to choose the bedroom decor coincided with their FA Cup-winning run of 1970, I gave Mum a Chelsea rosette so she could buy the wallpaper and bed covers in exactly the right colours. **❞**

IAN BOTHAM

1994

❝I actually don't look forward to Chelsea games these days because they've become real wars. **❞**

TOM 'LOFTY' WATT

writer, actor and Arsenal fan

" There's only one real Chelsea kit – the classic kit of the early 70s. The worst has to be the tangerine and grey. What the hell's that got to do with Chelsea? "

TIM LOVEJOY

TV presenter

❝I think we were meant to be in a state of continual frustration. I think it might upset everyone more than they know if we actually won something. **❞**

DAVID BADDIEL

September 1995

184

"Wisey would have made it as a scrum-half. He would have adapted and the game would have knocked that edge out of him.**"**

England rugby international **BRIAN MOORE**

"The fastest man at Stamford Bridge was Clive Walker. I raced him in a 60-metres dash. I won't tell you who won, but we were both dipping for the tape.**"**

SEB COE

April 1991

❝I've asked John Major if he's going to start coming again. He gets a bloody good pension as a former prime minister, so he might even be able to afford a season ticket. **❞**

TONY BANKS MP

July 1997

187

❝When I was at school, I preferred football to cricket. Until cricket took over, I'd play football on Saturday mornings and then go to watch Chelsea in the afternoons, standing in the Shed.**❞**

ALEC STEWART

September 1990

"I think cooking is like football.
It's not a job, it's a passion.
When you become good at it, it's a dream
job and financially you need never to
worry. Ever. **"**

GORDON RAMSAY

chef, restaurateur, writer and television personality

❝I am now a football fan. I know this because in one afternoon I learnt I'm not a football fan at all. I'm a fan of Chelsea. Chelsea are the only team that can play. Chelsea players have by far the most impressive reproductive organs. Stamford Bridge is my church. The men who play there are my gods.**❞**

JEREMY CLARKSON

writing in, "How Hard Can It Be? The World According to Clarkson"

❝I read a lot of things about Mason and I think he's a very underappreciated player – but not by us. **❞**

GARETH SOUTHGATE

praising Mason Mount after England beat Belgium in October 2020

"He's not running for Pope or sainthood; he's a footballer."

Respect MP **GEORGE GALLOWAY**
defends John Terry on BBC's Question Time, *February 2010*